Above & Beyond Wellfleet

A memoir about welcoming life after loss

Constance B. Wilder

A Tiny Tomes™ Publication

2012

Above and Beyond Wellfleet
Published by Tiny Tomes™
ISBN:978-0-9857050-2-2
First Edition

DEDICATED

TO

Katie and Rob, who are closest to my heart
and their families,
David, Sebastien, Ethan, Staci, and Bobby

DEDICATED IN MEMORY OF
My Parents
Richard and Frances Wilder
For their love and wisdom and no sleepovers*

TO
Dr. Jean L. Parker
My English Professor at Elmira College

To Binker
The closest to being human on four paws

AND
TO
Larry
"Always"

When my ten year old grandson, Ethan, read this dedication to my parents, he added after love and wisdom — and no sleepovers. He remembered a story I told about how my parents forbid me to go to slumber parties, because my lack of sleep made me too emotional.

CONTENTS

The Introduction

I started writing this book ten years ago. My black book (my journal) and I have been a familiar sight in many coffee shops, restaurants, and perhaps my favorite — writing from a blue Adirondack chair at The Studio in Friendship, Maine.

I've been mistaken for a food critic and people have stared at me. Who writes and eats at the same time? I do.

Right now, I am writing this introduction in the restaurant at the Emerson Inn By the Sea in Rockport, Massachusetts. In the mid-1850s, this Inn was the Pigeon Cove House; its most famous guest was Ralph Waldo Emerson.

The serendipity of writing under the same roof as the author of the essay, *Self Reliance*, is not lost on me. I'm struck by the coincidence of how many of the stories of my ten-year journey through grief have had to do with testing my self-reliance.

Tonight, I am dining with the kindred spirit of Mr. Emerson. As I am eating and writing, I am remembering a conversation I had with a friend, years ago, when we were discussing Emerson's famous essay. She said, "Did you know that he had dinner with his mother at least once a week?" My skeptical friend regarded the fact that Emerson still enjoyed the company of his mother, her care, and her hospitality as contrary to his beliefs about being self-reliant.

I believe my friend was wrong to poke holes in what Emerson was trying to say. Self-reliance is not solely depending on oneself to nurture personal well-being — far from it. The love of family and friends is at all times critical, especially when experiencing hard times.

Emerson, I believe, encouraged our getting to know ourselves. He asked us to know ourselves and to rely first on our own strengths.

Grieving is the supreme test in understanding ourselves.

While building strength after devastating loss, I wrote this book for others to lean on, hoping that the words will fill a void caused by loss. I hope it will be a companion, perhaps summoned in the middle of the night, at 3 a.m., which I call the universal hour of grief. It is in the middle of the night when family and friends are asleep that the terrors strike: the real or irrational fears, the list of worries, the pounding of a broken heart, and the weight of intense loneliness bearing down. My hope is that at that hour these pages will keep you company, helping you to know that while you are lonely, you are not alone.

What I share are personal stories. They have not been written to boast or to say smugly, "I can do it; so can you." I bare my heart to those I do not know because I am a fellow traveler.

Grief is lonely. Grief is unique. Grief is universal. Grief topples trust. Grief transforms. Grief can destroy faith.

As I write these statements, I wonder why it is mostly a secret subject. It's either avoided or dealt with in staccato-like conversations. I kept writing these last ten years because we've all lost someone dear to us. Yet while the experience is common, the treatment of the subject is almost always, at best, vague and superficial.

I went to a bookstore three days after my husband's funeral to find some books to read. I asked the store manager where the section on grief was. He looked bewildered, and brought me to what he thought was a logical section of the store. I found two books, written by widowed women describing their experiences. And, surprisingly, I found in the same section a book on how to live to be 100. I bought it and the other two.

These books became my comfort in the early days after losing my husband, even the one advising how to live a long life. These authors became friends whom I would never meet. They helped me to understand that I had a lot of work to do to try and understand how to cope with my loss.

All of this brings me back to self-reliance. I don't know exactly what Emerson was trying to teach us, but

I choose to believe that he did not mean we had to go through life's hard experiences alone. We can have dinner with our mother and our friends. We can rely on them for comfort and for companionship. But I also believe that he wanted us to test ourselves and to trust our instincts. He wanted us to get to know ourselves intimately.

Facing a tragic loss tears us to the bone. It is hard to know who we are anymore; we've been knocked off our gyroscope, tipped off balance because we have lost an integral part of our being. That is what love is all about: you cleave to the one you love and when they are physically gone, you are diminished, almost disappearing in the aftermath of that loss.

Love shouldn't be any other way: the greater the love, the greater the loss. Herculean strength is required to work your way out of the sadness. It is like walking through a dark tunnel, not knowing if there is light at the end of it.

The tunnel is filled with curves and bumps. There are guiding lights: some appear fortuitously and some are sought after. It's an emotional marathon, completed without training.

These stories represent my journey to the light at the end of the tunnel. There are still shadows. There are still memories that wrench. They've just become a part of the new me. I almost wrote "the improved me," but I'm not sure about that! At least I can report that I am a "whole me," no longer the diminished "me" who existed ten years ago.

I don't know you. But I do know your pain. I don't know how you feel. No one can. But I do know that there is strength within to keep us going.

My dinner companion tonight has the last words from his essay to help guide us:

> *"Trust thyself: every heart beats to that iron string."*
> RALPH WALDO EMERSON

The Painting

The flowers were frozen. The petals had faded, stems drooped, and a dusting of new-fallen snow covered the arrangement. The florist had placed them on the front step, obviously expecting that there would be someone home to bring them inside. I saw them out of the corner of my eye as I pulled into the driveway.

The outside house lights were not on. Of course they weren't; who would have turned them on? He always turned the lights on just before it got dark.

As I looked at the light fixtures, I thought about how much work had gone into renovating our two-hundred year old antique home: the home where we would spend our retirement. We had been particular about every detail, including hiring a Cape Cod craftsman to design the lights that were guaranteed for life. I remembered how impressed I was with the promise "guaranteed for life." I now almost chuckled at the gallows humor. Instead, I kept staring at the house.

The front windows, which at night used to glow like eyes, were dark, but I could still see the lighted church steeple across the street reflected in the living room window. For several months during that last year, an owl had taken up residence in the steeple. I thought his hoots were mournful. But he sang at night, which I, at least, found comforting, because I had heard that if you hear an owl during the day, it is bad luck.

We'd had enough bad luck.

Fearing an owl hooting during the day was easier to think about than it was to truly hear the words spoken in doctors' offices, starting with the diagnosis that I suspected had been delivered too late.

I sat in the car for several minutes, summoning the strength to go inside. I wanted to stay in the car, but I was getting cold.

Twilight faded; it was now dark. I clutched the keys in my hand and walked slowly to the door. The light snow made the walk and steps slippery. I paused by the frozen flowers. I considered taking them inside. Instead, I took the card. By the light of the church steeple I saw that my niece had sent the flowers as a thoughtful gesture.

Just as I opened the door, the church bells rang three times. "Three bells," I could hear my husband saying, "three bells — it's 5:30." The church was one of the few in the country that rang its bells in nautical time.

The sound of the chimes was replaced with the beeping of our alarm system warning me that I had seconds to enter the code, the four digits of our birth years.

The house was cold. I had been gone for two weeks arranging the final farewell. Before I left, I had turned down the thermostat to 50 degrees, following our house rules. Against the rules, I turned up the thermostat to 80 degrees to heat up the house quickly. Then I turned on the lights.

The emptiness was exposed now. I thought to myself, "What could I have done to prepare myself for the shock of being in this dark house alone?" Rather than think about the answer, I reverted to what had become my way of dealing with piercing emotion: I turned away from it.

I left the house and went back outside to get my suitcase. I walked carefully, but I nearly fell on the newly painted red steps. Several months before, we had painted the steps and the front door red. Ancient Chinese believed that the color red drove away misfortune. In my muddled state, I had believed that if we painted the steps and door red, everything would be all right.

I had few coping mechanisms at the time. Mythology was easier to grasp than were the doctors' predictions. Painting the door and the steps red was a cruel hoax played on a weary mind struggling to remain hopeful. We were fixated on hope.

I pulled my suitcase out of the car, and carried it to the front door. This suitcase was filled with black clothes that I would probably give away. I had a habit of giving away any clothes I'd worn when we received bad news.

When I got in the house, I locked the front door and set the suitcase down in the hall. I didn't have the strength to carry it to our bedroom. The word "our" stuck in my head like a dagger. Our house had become my house, and this new reality petrified me.

As I had done so often in the past four years, I slammed the door shut in my brain. Sometimes I imagined that a box inside my brain held my terror so tightly that my fears would never escape. The box was bursting as I stood in the hall of this cold and dark house. Some believe that love and hate are closely aligned. I never understood that; now I did. I loved this house, and now I had begun to hate it.

As I stood in the hall, trying to numb my brain from the siege of emotions, I felt new terrors. I was alone and vulnerable, and I was scared. A young mother had been murdered weeks before in the small Cape Cod town of Truro, one town beyond Wellfleet. The story had made national news. It was a particularly brutal murder, the first in Truro in many decades; no suspects had been arrested.

"Don't worry, you'll be safe." An echo was speaking.

Again, I questioned how I could have prepared myself for my return to the house. Should I have removed all the furniture? If I had, I would not have had to look at the dining room table and pictured family and friends gathered around it as we laughed away the inevitable sadness that hung around us like a clinging spider web.

I would not have seen the two chairs in front of the fireplace — I called it our winter bistro — one of which would now remain permanently empty. The gentleman's chair was his chair in the small room where we watched television. What should I do with that?

"Come watch this touchdown," the echo was speaking again.

I had so much to learn. In an attempt to see my future, I would write in my journal. It held my sadness and my secrets. One particularly scary night, I crept downstairs, never waking him, and lit a candle. I sat down in one of the bistro chairs. I couldn't find my journal, but I found a small notebook I'd left on the kitchen counter that contained healthy recipes I had collected for my husband. I turned to the first empty page and, with a shaky hand, started to write. I poured my breaking heart onto these pages, for the first time admitting that the battle was probably lost.

I wrote for several hours. I pried open just a crack in the box in my head, letting out my deepest fears. I remember the date, December 16, 2001, a day that would live in my personal infamy. I had let out two unthinkable truths: The first was that my husband's courageous battle was nearly over. The second was that soon I would be learning to live alone, something I had never done in 55 years. The admissions were too much. I ripped out the pages, rumpled them in a tight little ball and quietly buried them in the kitchen rubbish bin.

Now, standing in the house, I was beginning to experience the learning-to-live-alone truth written that dark night as I took in the stark emptiness around me.

I was alone, but the house was full, crammed with memories, accentuating how empty it was.

We had filled the house with love. We had honored its past. We had carefully restored it, so that we could spend our retirement years here, creating our own history. The house was situated on top of one of the highest hills in Wellfleet on the outer Cape. We were told by a local historian that it was originally built on one of the islands in Wellfleet but the owner was fearful of flood tides, so he had the original structure moved by a team of horses to the highest point in town.

The house was safe. I tried to breathe in that comfort, as my eyes took in the bleakness that surrounded me. I mused, "Can this house protect me and make me feel safe again?"

I was exhausted so I forced myself to climb the stairs to the bedroom. When I walked in, I felt exposed. All the shades were up.

I went to the window overlooking Main Street and saw a man walking on the sidewalk. It was Wellfleet and it was winter; the sidewalks were normally empty, especially at night. He looked up. Did he see me? I yanked down the shade thinking, "Could this be the killer of the young mother?" At the same time, I wondered if these thoughts were going to become a part of my new life — being suspicious of any stranger walking on the sidewalk after dark.

I raced to reset the alarm and asked the house to keep me safe. Had I fooled myself? I thought the house, our retirement home, situated between an historic church and a harbor, would be my sanctuary. Instead, the house was chilled by love lost, darkened by loneliness, tainted by terror, and filled with dreams sabotaged.

I felt frozen by fear; I questioned whether I would ever again be happy in this house, a place where my husband's voice was an echo and his face a mirage. The house was the embodiment of him. Was it possible to integrate myself into it? Would the house accept just me?

—⁂—

My husband died on January 31, 2002, just as the new year had begun.

My melancholy made me question whether all of my new years would be cursed. I thought coming back to our house would make me stronger. Instead, it made me feel weak.

I worked hard over the next several months to make friends with the house. But each day we quarreled. I moved furniture and put away photographs. I tried to preserve the past, but pushed the house into the present. It wouldn't budge. I couldn't make the house happy.

I tried to ignore the fact that the house controlled my life. I began each day trying to win its favor. How did this contest begin? Who was in charge? The house had an unhealthy hold on me. As much as my heart ached, missing my husband, I began to realize that I could not live in his shrine.

I sometimes went to a Wellfleet coffee shop at the crack of dawn, trying to figure out if I could fit into this town. It was late February. Wellfleet's population fluctuates dramatically from summer to winter. After Columbus Day, there is almost a seismic whoosh of people exiting, shops closing, and traffic dwindling.

The winters are desolate. If you have a companion to share the fireside, it is hardly noticeable. If you don't, being alone can be crushing. I had returned home alone to Wellfleet in winter.

I came to the Outer Cup coffee shop to be with people and to hear the locals banter. I would sit alone at a table with my journal, drinking coffee, and writing. While my husband and I owned a house in Wellfleet, we were not members of the community. We had created our own community with family and friends.

One morning, I walked into the coffee shop and noticed a beautiful watercolor painting by Traci Harmon (Traci Harmon-Hay) that had just been hung in the entrance; it was for sale. The image was of the town of Wellfleet bathed in an ice blue with our house in the center.

Above the town was a floating house, its windows glowing with warmth. The contrast between the beautiful little floating house and the icy stillness of the town below struck me instantly. I saw my husband in the floating house — safe, warm, peaceful and happy. My mind went inside the house and pictured him in this new place; I even imagined him sitting and warming himself by the fireplace that made the windows glow.

The painting forced me to see that my husband had moved away from me. He had a new house. This remarkable painting also made me see that I was not free. I was in our house, frozen and captive.

The title of the painting was "Above Wellfleet." I bought it. It had given me a personal epiphany. It is the painting on the cover of this book.

Months later, against most advice, I startled family and friends by selling the house. It was a decision viewed by some that I was selling a piece of my husband. They were right. He was an integral part of the house. This painting, however, allowed me to understand that he no longer lived there, nor did his spirit.

As I drove out of the driveway for the last time, clutching the steering wheel, surprisingly I did not cry. I was sad thinking about what could have been, but I concentrated on believing that my husband had a new home, and I was headed to mine.

The Hope

Selling the house freed me to start a new life, but it did not free me from grieving and trying to understand my loss.

I was removed from the place where I felt shackled by memories, but they were still there. I could not escape the inevitable grieving process that lay ahead of me.

Three months before my husband died, I was hospitalized with a severe case of diverticulitis. Several weeks after I was released, the pain returned. I could not be hospitalized again; my husband was too weak to be left alone. As I sat waiting in the examining room of our local clinic, I started staring at a poster on the wall advertising antidepressants. A series of questions were posed on this poster. One of the questions was, "Have you ever felt like ending your life?" At that moment, I was as desperate and in as much pain as I had ever been. I knew I was about to experience a huge loss, but I involuntarily shook my head "no," answering that question.

Hope was still deep within me, but it was shifting away from my husband's survival to my own. Did I know that my hope was evolving at that time? I'm fairly certain I did not; in reality, and with the benefit of ten years' perspective, I knew I still felt hopeful.

We had a magnet on our refrigerator that read, "Where there's life, there's hope." Perhaps it was hope that was the guiding force that fueled our taking advantage of every medical option offered to my husband to cure his cancer. He was diagnosed at a risky stage of melanoma. He was a brave, optimistic, and cheerful man. He never lost hope, and if he ever did, he never revealed it.

Because he was courageous, those who loved him followed his lead. We all managed to match his smile and we dug deeply to feel his optimism. He never cried about his circumstance, and the only time I cried was in the shower so I could blame my red eyes on soap.

Did I ever lose hope? I have to admit I was sorely tested. In the four-year battle with his disease, he endured an initial seven-hour surgery requiring three skin grafts; a year of Interferon treatment (which left him almost bedridden for a year); two separate lymph node surgeries; two different series of brain radiation treatments; three clinical trials; and numerous MRIs, CTs and PET scans.

With each treatment, I hoped and prayed it would be the one that would save my husband's life. That kind of hope does not allow room for doubt. If it had a chance of curing my husband, we did it. I say "we," because while he endured the physical effects of the treatments, I was his medical partner. In four years, I rarely missed a doctor's appointment, I was in every surgery waiting room, I sat beside him for the year of his every-other-day self-administered shot of Interferon, and I researched every possible nutritional advantage to support his struggle.

In many ways, his life became my life; his survival was my primary goal. His hope for a happy ending was my hope.

With our unhappy ending, now where would I put my hope? That was the shift: with one hope dashed, a new hope had to take its place.

The Ants

Have you ever seen a colony of ants carrying one of its injured on the back of one, with the others clustered around to help support the effort? That is what our family and friends did for us. They carried us on their backs. One member of their colony was injured and they did everything they could to help make our situation easier. They made the medical maze bearable.

What did they do?

They made soup.

They made ice cream.

They drove to doctors' appointments.

They sat in doctors' offices and in surgery waiting rooms.

They gave telephone money cards (cell phones at the time were forbidden in the hospital, for fear that they could interfere with medical equipment).

They made a bedroom in their homes, for us.

They traveled long distances just to give a reassuring hug.

They helped sort out complex legal and medical issues.

They never left us alone in our fear and they stayed in the hardest place of all when they knew the battle was lost.

They never left us behind.

All of these were generous acts of love. Because they laughed with us, they swept away the sadness when it tried to overcome us. They held their tears until it was time for them to flow.

We were grateful for every loving gesture. And while my husband and I were humbled by them all, there were two that were remarkable.

One occurred after my husband had finished his year-long Interferon treatment, which laid low a man who had always had boundless energy. During this year he struggled each day to get out of bed. It was so debilitating that he would have to take a two-hour nap after he shaved so that he could get dressed and go to the office for an hour.

He limped across the finish line as he took his last shot, and he felt triumphant.

My daughter felt that that feat should be celebrated with a special occasion. She raised this idea with very good friends asking them, "Do you think we could secretly contact other friends and ask them to contribute to a trip to a bed and breakfast?" Our friend said, "Hell, we can do more than that! Let's send them to Europe." And a brilliant, secret plan was hatched. My mother said, "If you don't get enough contributions, I'll cover the shortfall."

Enough was contributed to send my husband and me to Paris and Provence for a week and a half. All of this was done without our having a clue.

A second memory rushes into my mind. We had been visiting friends in Rochester, NY, where we lived before moving to the Cape. Before meeting a friend for coffee one afternoon, I visited my favorite library. I couldn't help always checking the Internet to see if there was something new I needed to know about melanoma. Unfortunately, I came across an article citing the survival statistics for the stage of my husband's disease. They were grim. I was shaken. I met my friend and couldn't hide my worry. I shared just a bit of what I had just read. She was comforting.

The next week, she sent me a card with a gift enclosed. On the card she wrote that she had just made herself the President-CEO of a new company called Tiny Treasures. I was its only customer. Every month for almost two years, until my husband passed away, she sent me a card and a small gift. Every day, I take a vitamin from one of those tiny gifts. It is a small ceramic pot and when it is empty, you see the words "I miss you."

Some memories of the four years of my husband's illness are hard to keep. But the love and kindness we were shown make them bearable.

Just like the ants who take care of their own and never leave a fallen friend behind, our family and friends always kept us close to their hearts and carried us through many an emotional minefield. They are still there for me. Each day I thank them in my prayers; I hope they hear them.

The Bed

My husband died at 5:30 AM. There were several very hard days leading up to that tragic hour, starting with the day I had to call our hospice caretaker and ask that a hospital bed be delivered to the house.

The night before I made the call, Larry woke up in the middle of the night needing to go to the bathroom. I'd been able to manage these visits with him, but I barely could this time. He was so weak; he could hardly stand. He leaned on me as we walked to the bathroom. On the way back to the bedroom, he staggered and hit his head on the molding of our bedroom door. He nearly fell again before I could get him back to bed. His body was "shutting down." What an awful term that is, but that is what I was told would happen. And it was happening.

The next morning, when the hospital bed arrived, I was asked if Larry could walk downstairs to where the bed was being placed. No, he could not. I wanted the hospital bed placed in our dining room in front of our sliding doors so that he could still have the view of the marsh and harbor.

When hospice realized that we needed help to get Larry downstairs, they called the Fire Department. I thought by this time that I knew most of the angels on Earth, but I was about to meet two more. Two burly firemen arrived, carrying a narrow wooden chair. I brought them upstairs to our bedroom. They went over to Larry and gently began to describe how they were going to put him in the chair and take him downstairs. Larry nodded trustingly.

I asked that they wait for a moment before taking him downstairs so I could put a pair of socks on him. They were hand knitted socks that we bought in Nova Scotia on our last vacation together. I didn't want his feet to be cold. When I finished putting his socks on, Larry took my hand and said "Thank you." I believe those were the last words he said to me; once he got in the hospital bed, the end was very near.

After he got settled in the bed, I went upstairs to get his pillow and blanket. I walked into the bedroom, took one look at the bed and knew I would never sleep in it again. I called a mover several hours later and had the bed moved out of our bedroom.

———⁌⁃⁌———

On the morning my husband died, two dear friends arrived mid-morning to help field condolence calls and to stand guard in the kitchen to get me anything I needed.

I was in our den making arrangements. My friends would open the door to the den from time to time and ask me if I wanted anything. Usually, I asked for more tea. At 2:30 the door opened. My friend asked what I needed, and I responded by saying "I need a bed." She shut the door, but reopened it quickly. She said, "Did you say you needed a bed?" I said, "Yes."

I explained that I no longer had a bed in the bedroom, and I needed a bed.

These friends would have done anything for me. As bizarre as this request was, she kept the conversation going. "Where should we look for this bed?"

There aren't many furniture stores on Cape Cod, and there certainly weren't any in Wellfleet. For some reason (this whole story is serendipitous) I said "I think there is a gift shop next door to that place where we have lunch in Dennis." Did I know the name of the shop? No, I did not. But I suggested that my friend call the restaurant and get the name. About fifteen minutes later, she opened the door again with the most amazed look on her face. She said, "You are not going to believe this; I called the gift shop and they have one bed — it's a double bed, it's iris blue and the owner just put it on sale." I said "Here's my credit card; please buy the bed." My friend insisted that I leave the den and come with them. "You need to get out of here and see the bed."

I followed my friends out the door and crawled into the back seat of their car, shivering. The day was as it should have been: cold, dark, and stormy. While my friends chatted in the front seat, I watched the rain slap against the window.

When we walked into the shop, the owner, whom I had never met, greeted me with a hug; she had been told the story. Just as I was paying for the bed, her husband came into the shop. She went over to him and whispered something. She came back and said to me, "My husband will deliver the bed to you tonight."

My friends stepped in and said, "That will be great. Now we have to go and find a mattress; we'll be in touch."

It was 4:30, but my friends were undeterred. We arrived at the mattress store just as it was about to close. My friends breezed in and gave the order for what I needed. It was January and it was Cape Cod so the manager was actually happy to be making a sale. I picked out a mattress and box spring and my friend said that we had to call someone to pick them up. "Oh," said the manager, "you can't have this mattress set. It will have to come from the warehouse." "Where's the warehouse?" my friend asked. "Hyannis, but you can't have this set today."

My friends are determined people and they told the man the story, making it quite clear that I needed the mattress and box spring TODAY. The manager made a call, kept the warehouse open, and my friends called the husband who was delivering the bed and who also went to pick up the mattress set at the warehouse in Hyannis.

By 7:30 that night, fourteen hours after my husband died, my new bed was assembled by my son, and made up with fresh sheets by my friends. I still sleep in that bed, and every night I relive that memory — a memory which lifted my spirits on what was possibly the saddest day of my life.

The Good News, the Bad News

Building on gratitude and seeking a new hope, I went through a metamorphosis. Did I go through a personality change? I don't think so. But I did change. I had to. The construct of my life was completely different, and I had to figure out how to fit into it.

The good news was that I only had myself to consider when making decisions. The bad news was that I only had myself to consider when making decisions.

This new freedom was invigorating and lonely. I liked the collaborative decision-making process that I had enjoyed with my husband, but I had to admit to myself that there hadn't been much of that in those last four years. Cancer dictated most of our decisions and what it did not dictate, my husband did, because he had the most to gain and the most to lose from every decision we made.

I was forced to find a new partner — a new collaborator — one I could trust and one in whom I could confide my deepest fears and questions.

My instincts became my new partner. They led the way in a manner I'm not sure I had ever experienced. Selling the Cape house was the first instance of listening to what my gut was telling me. By making such a major decision, I went against the first universal piece of advice given to someone suffering significant loss: I made an almost immediate, irreversible decision. I did it because it felt wrong to be where I was living, and even though I didn't know where the right place was, something gave me the confidence that I would find it.

This new partnership caused me to wrap myself in a cocoon so tightly that I let few people inside. As an example, directly after my husband's funeral, I went away for five days to grieve in a hotel that had been important to both of us. Many didn't understand why I did this. My family and friends wanted to comfort me, but I instinctively knew that I would miss him more being with other people who knew us as a couple than I would be by myself.

That first foray of listening to my inner voice was just what I needed to get reacquainted with someone who had become a stranger: me. For a long time I hadn't really known what I wanted, what I needed, and what I required to make my life whole. Something was compelling me to answer those questions.

This rediscovery caused ruptures in some relationships. I pushed people away who needed my help and comfort, but I found I had little to give. Grief had hollowed me.

My reserves were spent. I devoted what little energy I had to getting to know this emerging person. I focused my attention on anything that allowed me to sense that I might have a future without my husband.

It was ironic. I was 55 years old and I was alone for the first time in my life. Instead of seeking the comforting companionship of family and friends, I let only a few people be a part of my life. Those who understood that I was going through a painful metamorphosis were let in; those who didn't were not. It was a hell of a time to go through a growth spurt. My behavior was a mystery to others and surprising to me.

I tried to explain myself to those who didn't understand and who questioned my decisions. Somehow, I garnered the strength that prevented me from changing course just to suit how others wanted me to be. Instead of lining up people with whom I could share my grief, I kept testing my stamina to see how many experiences I could endure alone.

I look back at those early years, and I am grateful that I listened so carefully to my own instincts of what I needed to do to abandon one dream and to hold close to another. My dream of growing old with my husband had been sabotaged. My new dream was to create a life where I could still appreciate the beauty and love that surrounded me.

I was first married at 21, two weeks after being graduated from college. Our first child was born when I was 22 and our second when I was 25. I was divorced when I was 34 and I remarried when I was 37. Until my husband died, I had never walked into an empty home and have it remain that way for long. Either a parent or husband or child would walk through the door. At 55, my nest was starkly empty.

The challenge was to balance the fear that came with the freedom. On the plus side, the remote was mine, the time for dinner was mine to determine, the places to visit were my choices, the speed at which the car traveled was mine to decide, but those were such meager bonuses to balance having lost loving companionship. The only answer for me was to figure out, slowly and steadily, what this new life was all about. When something worked, it was exhilarating. When something didn't, I was as frightened as I had ever been in my life.

Each step I took deepened the bond between my instincts and me. It turns out that they know me best. I rarely argue with them these days. If something feels right, I do it. If it doesn't feel right, I don't do it. It's really that simple.

The New Beginning

A fluttering of new hope got stronger as I sat in a restaurant in Quebec City, Canada. I was on a sojourn, traveling to escape celebrating the first Thanksgiving eleven months after Larry died. I couldn't face it without him at the head of the table. My heart turned to ice when I saw the first signs of the approaching holidays. I was seized with a whole new sadness.

My solution was to run away from home.

I decided to test my traveling-solo wings, and I needed to get away from the traditions: traditions I had previously loved, but that now tore at me. Canadians celebrate Thanksgiving in October, so the timing of my November escape was perfect.

I arrived in Quebec City in a wind-driven snowstorm. As I fought my way through the blinding snow I thought of a comment a friend had made when I told her where

I was going. She asked if I'd heard of Florida where the sun would be shining and I could walk on a beach. Yes, the sun shines in Florida but people will be celebrating Thanksgiving. Braving the snowstorm versus seeking the sun turned out to be providential.

Quebec City was magical. I arrived just as the city was getting ready for the holidays. Festive decorations and twinkling lights were everywhere. I felt as if I had been transported to another time and place, which was just what my aching heart needed. The atmosphere made me happy, mostly because none of it was familiar. That's the tricky part of grieving and the key to coping: at painful times, it is best to be in new places where memories do not haunt.

The beginning of new hope was fully felt several days after I arrived, when I looked out the window of a restaurant where I was having lunch; I was testing onion soup. I had decided to make onion soup reviews a part of my nightly emails to friends and family who were following my travels.

The gallery owner across the street from the restaurant was arranging his holiday decorations in window boxes. They were two large gingerbread cutouts: a boy and a girl, each trimmed with green piping and surrounded with a cluster of fresh greens. The sight of them made me smile broadly. My frozen heart was melting. Those two gingerbread people broke through a hardened crust of ice.

I've thought about that moment and wondered why those two whimsical characters began to change my acceptance of the holidays and became the symbol of a burgeoning recognition that I could, once again, feel happiness.

I've come to believe that the boy and the girl reminded me of my children.

Katie and Rob always helped me to survive hardship. They were the reason I recovered from a dark divorce, and I called on that love as I faced another loss. They were my foundation.

I was careful to treat that foundation with respect, knowing that it would be unfair to them and unhealthy for me to have them feel my heavy weight as I rebuilt my life.

This rebuilding caused a dramatic change in the way others saw me, and the way in which I saw myself. I still cared deeply for my close family and friends, but what was beginning to emerge was a deep concern for my own well being.

For most of my life I had been viewed as a dedicated caretaker of others. This new beginning caused a shift in my thinking; I started to care for myself first and others second, a sensible theory. However, it was pointed out to me that I didn't put this theory into practice very often.

Several months after Larry died, I was handed a piece of paper by a therapist who probably saved my sanity. On the paper was written the definition of the word "boundary." It read, "You cannot simultaneously take care of another person's feelings and set a boundary for yourself."

Really? I was floored. It seemed completely selfish to me. She helped me to understand that if I didn't take care of my own needs and health, I would hurt myself and become a burden to others.

It was not an easy habit to break, but I've gotten quite good at living that definition. At one point during Larry's illness, I was too exhausted to go on a planned trip. He went without me. A friend said to me several weeks later, "That was so unlike you, Connie." It was so unlike me — she was right. I now understand that it was the best thing I could have done. I was running on empty, and I needed to recharge my batteries.

In the course of building a new beginning, I have worked hard to create an "unlike Connie." I haven't abandoned all of the old Connie, but I have made a fundamental change to care for myself first — not selfishly — but protectively.

The Ring

The marriage that was ended by my husband's death was a second marriage for both of us. Each of us had experienced painful divorces.

Divorce is a death, but the regret and sorrow it causes does not die. Children and partners are hurt irrevocably and a certain innocence is lost forever.

Because of the pain caused by each of our marriages dissolving, we vowed to each other to be grateful for another chance at lasting love. The saying, "You don't know what you've got until it's gone" did not apply to us. We appreciated every day what we had.

We planned a simple wedding. As a part of the preparation, we had decided to have a friend design our wedding bands. When we went to see him, we had ideas as to what we wanted. He knew us well. He acknowledged that we probably had our own designs that we wanted to show him, but asked if he could share his idea with us first. We agreed.

He said (I am remembering this as if it happened yesterday), "You are both busy people, each involved in your careers and raising families, but I sense an unusual closeness between you, and I would like to design rings for you that will allow you to be together even when you are apart." We never offered our ideas after hearing that sentence.

The rings he designed for us were almost identical except for one difference. Each was a gold curved band; the difference was on the back of each ring. On my husband's was my fingerprint from the finger on which I would wear the ring; on the back of my ring was my husband's fingerprint.

When he died 19 years later, I found that each of our fingerprints had been rubbed smooth. Our goldsmith friend was right. My wedding ring was my amulet. I would unconsciously rub it when I missed my husband or when I was afraid. There were times in the middle of the night after his cancer was diagnosed when I would wake up startled and feel my heart beating in the pit of my stomach. Rubbing his fingerprint soothed my panic. Although he never admitted to feeling panicked, my fingerprint on his ring had completely disappeared by the time he died.

Whenever he had a scan or surgery, he had to take off his wedding ring. I would wear both, putting his on first and using mine as a guard so it wouldn't fall off. After the test or as the anesthesia was wearing off, he would immediately ask for his ring back.

When he left our house for the last time, I could not bear to watch him "go" out the door. I went upstairs. When I came back down, his wedding band had been placed in the middle of the dining room table. I took mine off, put his on and used mine as a guard. Knowing that he would not be asking for it back was excruciating.

I wore the two rings for months, but it didn't feel right. I couldn't stand to wear them that way, but I couldn't stand to let them go, so I put them on a gold chain and wore them as a necklace. That arrangement lasted about a year. They still made me sad. I put them away in my jewelry box.

I missed them. They weren't jewelry; they were symbols of an abiding love. One day, I lifted the lid of the box and saw them staring at me. I asked myself what I was saving them for. I couldn't wear them, I couldn't part with them, and I couldn't see how they would be appropriate family heirlooms since the luster of love had been tarnished by sadness.

An idea sprouted. I could have them melted down and made into one ring. Fortunately, I knew just the person to approach with my idea. I brought the rings to a creative jeweler in Newburyport. I told him the story. His eyes showed me he understood what I was trying to do. He asked how I wanted it designed. For the second time in the life of these rings, I left it up to the jeweler to do the design. As I handed them over to him, he took a deep breath and said, "I will do something that you will love."

When he showed me the ring, I was the one who could hardly breathe. I held in my hand a gold band about ⅛ of an inch wide, studded with tiny diamonds and pink sapphires. The jeweler said he wanted me to think of stars when I looked at it. Along with the ring, he handed me a small plastic box in which was some sort of mottled nugget. He could see I had no idea what it was. He said, "Connie, that is the leftover gold." This young man was talented and trustworthy. I never would have known that there was left-over gold. I asked him if he could make something out of it. Yes, he could. He designed what looked to me like a tear-drop studded with even tinier diamonds and sapphires. It became a beautiful addition to my charm bracelet.

I wear the gold wedding band and the teardrop charm every day.

Another change had taken place. When I wore the two wedding rings, I was reminded of love lost. With one ring made from the melted bands, I am reminded of love honored.

The Parents

My father was dead and my mother was 90 when I started my journey through grief, and yet they played a major role in giving me the courage to heal.

How? Because they gave me my backbone. They gave me my faith that surviving hardship is possible. And they filled me with the capacity to revere life even in its bleakest hour.

My mother and father divorced their spouses and married each other in the mid-1940s. I was the only child from their marriage, but I shared life with four half siblings, two sons from my mother's former marriage and a son and a daughter from my father's. We were a complicated family, but we were close.

The age differences between my brothers and sister and me were 9, 11, and 13 years. I also have a half-sister who is severely retarded whom I met only once many years ago.

I was the only child at home full time from the age of nine. I might have been spoiled had it not been for the fact that my brilliant father was also too trusting. His faith in the wrong people resulted in a series of unsuccessful business ventures that led to many years of family financial upheaval.

I could have been damaged by these experiences. Instead, I was exposed to lessons on how to successfully manage failure and disappointment. I was nourished by two parents who, no matter what was seriously going wrong in their lives, never made me feel as if the world were shaking under my feet. I felt secure when I could have felt intensely the opposite.

I wasn't oblivious to our circumstances. We moved from a large, beautiful home when I was eight years old to a walk-up tenement in the same town, where everyone knew our name. We moved to the tenement instead of to a house we had been offered on the outskirts of town so that I could continue to go to the same school. My parents shrugged off the shame they could have felt when some of their so-called good friends shunned them.

Lesson Number One: Don't shrink from a significant change in social status; ignore the slights and don't wilt in the face of worry.

We moved five times in ten years. My father won and lost a series of jobs. Bad business luck seemed to follow him. At one point for a short time, we lived on money he earned from several of his inventions. He may have been down on his luck, but his fertile mind was never fallow. During these tumultuous years, my parents accepted responsibility for a $100,000 debt caused by one of the business failures. It is mind-boggling to me to contemplate what that amount is in today's dollars; it was a staggering figure in the mid-1950s. They never considered filing for bankruptcy. It took years, but they repaid every penny.

Wherever we moved, they always chose the best school district for me, which meant a very narrow choice of the homes that we could afford. No matter how relatively common they were, my mother made each one beautiful.

They were all memorable, but I particularly remember a garden apartment in Connecticut situated on Long Island Sound. The interiors of all the apartments were identical and many families organized their furniture in the same way. There was an alcove next to the kitchen. All of our neighbors put their dining room sets in that alcove. But my parents put their dining room table in front of the window facing the ocean, giving us a water view at every meal. They arranged two overstuffed chairs in the alcove with an ottoman in between. On the wall next to the chairs they placed two bookcases, each with wide shelves that they used as side tables. I can still see my parents sitting in those chairs, talking life over. My mother's design talent gave us a sense of beauty and calm wherever we lived. She never let our financial disarray enter the door.

Lesson Number Two: No matter the circumstance, feather your nest with love and dignity.

In addition to leaving me that legacy, they taught me that failure is a relative term and that giving up in the face of it is never an option. My father's favorite poem was Rudyard Kipling's "IF." Each line is a clarion call on how to live an honorable life. All resonated poignantly with my father. For him, they were not just perfectly put together lines of poetry; he also lived some many times over. This one in particular comes to mind:

> *"If you can make one heap of all your winnings*
> *And risk it on one turn of pitch-and-toss,*
> *And lose, and start again at your beginnings*
> *And never breathe a word about your loss;"*

My father did not gamble on games; he gambled on the virtue of others. The only person he breathed his loss to was my mother. When times were tough, they didn't shield me from the reality; they simply protected me by teaching me what mattered in living a proper life:

It mattered that you held your head high even if you had been bowed by the weight of disappointment. It mattered that you were honest with yourself and with others. It mattered that you put your family first. Above all, it mattered that you were grateful for each day, no matter how hard it came down.

My father's luck finally changed in my early adolescence. His brilliance was recognized by a major corporation and he earned a good and stable income until he retired. Life was easier.

My parents are not alive to read these words. Their physical absence is a great loss for me, but they always sit on my shoulders, whispering their words of wisdom in my ears.

One piece of wisdom is branded on my brain. The words may not be original to my parents, but they lived them and passed them on. They are my gift to you, dear reader.

Lesson Number Three: "You put bad steel in the fire, it melts. You put good steel in the fire, it gets stronger."

My parents always made me feel like good steel.

The Journal

My mother used to say to me in troubled times, "talk about your feelings, even if just to a stone." I know the quotation was not original to her. I always thought it was biblical, but I cannot find the derivation; I just know that she was advising me to find a way to sort out my feelings.

My journal is my stone. Over the past ten years, it has become my constant companion. I take it to dinner; I take it to the beach. I talk to it early in the morning; I talk to it late at night.

This companionship developed late in my husband's battle with cancer. For years, hope overruled despair. The first time that hope gave way to honesty was a month and a half before my husband died. He was failing. He was rapidly losing weight and strength. We both knew the end was near, but loving conversations about the inevitable were mostly in code. My heart was breaking for him and for me. We were surrounded by family and friends whose hearts were breaking too.

When I admitted to my journal that the end was near, Larry had recently concluded a third clinical trial. It wasn't successful. His cancer was overpowering his body, like an invading demon that had taken control. As much as we did not want our fears confirmed, we knew we had to schedule an appointment with his doctor.

Giving up was not in our DNA. We fought to win— especially my husband. If the odds were great, he was inspired. If he were told that something was unachievable, he achieved it. He rarely lost a client or an election, and now he was facing losing the biggest challenge of all: saving his life.

The day after I made the appointment to see his doctor for the following week (scheduled right before Christmas), I woke up at four in the morning, barely able to breathe. I needed to talk with someone about how frightened I was, but the only person I could talk to was lying next to me and he had to be ten times more frightened than I was.

I've written about this in an earlier story. It was such an epic moment that it bears repeating.

My mind was racing; I thought my thumping heart would wake my husband. I needed to get out of bed.

I slowly moved the sheets back. I got out of bed. Stepping on the floor, I prayed that our 200-year-old floorboards would not creak under my feet. I crept downstairs. This night, in front of a flickering candle, I wrote in my small spiral notebook, "Larry is going to die."

I can hardly write those words 10 years later without trembling. For the next hour, I wrote my heart out until the arriving dawn made the candle unnecessary. I blew out the candle, read what I had written crumpled up the pages and threw them away. I snuck back upstairs and slid under the covers.

I had a huge secret, one I shared with only one companion: a notebook. The man who knew all my secrets had been denied this one. I trusted paper and pen more than my partner. I wondered whether I had just committed an act of betrayal or a powerful act of love, sparing my best friend.

It was both. I betrayed the honesty that had been the hallmark of our relationship. At the same time, my powerful act of love shielded him from the blunt acknowledgement of his fate.

My journal knew our marriage was doomed and that his disease was going to end it.

Six days later, his doctor took away the secret I'd been hiding when he said, "Larry, there is nothing more I can do for you; it is time to call hospice."

From that point on, my journal became my confidant. I told it then and I tell it now my secrets, my fears, my observations, my worries, my accomplishments, and my failures.

Does it know me better than I know myself? Maybe it knows me sooner than I know myself.

I write with abandon in my journal. I don't worry about offending; I don't concern myself with making a good impression; I don't look for answers. I just put on paper what comes into my head and from my heart.

When memories claw at my mind, I sort them out on my pages. The process helps me to understand which to keep and which ones to toss.

Sometimes what I write in my journal surprises me. I often read something I've written and mentally note, "I didn't know you felt that way." My journal has become my constant collaborator; it primes my instincts. I have developed the habit of writing down pros and cons of a significant issue in my journal; the process usually results in a disciplined decision.

When I look back over the last ten years, my journal knew first every important decision I have made. The most startling was when I made the decision to sell the Cape house.

It knows my small and big decisions. It also knows the most mundane parts of my life. Should I keep being a blonde or go natural? Do I really want another love relationship or am I content in being single and independent? Should I stop wearing skirts? Those are the "Dear Diary" questions I sometimes explore.

Then there are the other questions. What do I need to do to remain physically and financially secure? What relationships mean the most to me and how can I nurture them? What does my future hold?

I write about the silly and the serious. I write freely with whatever comes into my head. It is a magnificent freedom.

Some of what I've written has been fodder for this book. Some of the pages are stashed in boxes, for later reference, and some are to be thrown away.

What I know is this: my journal is my trusted friend and my "stone."

The Half a Pair of Scissors

My grandmother was a widow for over 50 years. Her husband, Solon Wilder, was 39 when he died, leaving his young wife, Edith, alone with my 11-year-old father and his younger brother. By all accounts, my grandfather was a remarkably brilliant and kind man. His wife was also remarkable.

She is one of my heroes. She lost the love of her life just as they were beginning to raise their family. His death cut short the rich romance they shared and denied my father and his brother the opportunity to be guided by his wisdom. I know my grandfather was wise and had a wonderful sense of humor. I know this because my grandmother kept him "alive" by telling us stories about him. I never saw my grandmother cry when she told her stories about Solon; her bravery always impressed me.

She began her early married life experiencing tragedy. Their first child died before she was a year old. She told me once that when my father was born (her second child) she had him sleep in a bassinette by her side of the bed and would wake up frequently during the night and put her fingers under his nose to make sure he was breathing.

Between the years of losing her husband and dying at 94, she raised two accomplished sons, established various homes for her family, and secured, for future generations, a cottage on the coast of Maine that was built by my great-grandfather at the turn of the century. Because of her foresight and fortitude, my grandchildren are the sixth generation to be privileged to create summer memories in this wonderful cottage.

My grandmother lived a single life from 1922 to 1978. She was a very dignified woman who knew my grandfather was "a hard act to follow," which is why I am sure she never remarried.

Was it difficult for her to be a single woman, raising two sons and being in charge of her life in the mid-1920s? It must have been. Not only did she come to grips with these challenges alone, but she did so in a day and age when single women were an anomaly.

She did admit to my mother that when she was in the company of couples on social occasions, she often felt like "a half pair of scissors."

That expression, which my mother repeated to me many years ago, somehow stuck in my memory. It was an incisive description of what it feels like to be a single person in a social world largely populated by couples.

I concentrated on that phrase when I was learning how to adjust to my life alone. As much as I wanted to emulate my grandmother's courage and strength, I resisted the image of feeling like "a half a pair for scissors," because I knew a half a pair of scissors couldn't cut it (or anything).

Being single isn't easy. Hotels rent "double occupancy" rooms as the standard. Dining alone in a restaurant almost inevitably brings "just you, then..." from the host or hostess. That phrase always makes me feel like "a half a pair of scissors."

One night I decided to go out to dinner in the restaurant in a hotel in which I was staying. It was Valentine's Day (you can imagine how I love that holiday). I did not want to have dinner in my room. I walked into the restaurant, gave my name for the reservation, received the quizzical look from the maître D and was seated. My server, Steve, introduced himself and asked if there would be anyone joining me. I said "No." He said "Oh, good, it will just be you and me tonight." He wasn't being fresh or forward. He was treating the situation sensitively, just as I had hoped he would.

It might be hard to imagine how these things make the single person feel diminished. All single people may be offended, but for the person grieving, it is painful. The slights may not be intentional, but they are there, just the same.

My grandmother and I shared a difficult adjustment when we lost our husbands. We joined a social world where, more often than not, we were foreigners. Were our experiences different from 1922 to 2002? I don't think so. Not only did we have to learn to cope with a singleness that we did not choose, but we had to experience a world where people do not know how to speak the language of grief.

The Weekends

I was watching one of my favorite British shows, *Murder in Suburbia*, which features two single women police detectives. The dialogue between them is usually wonderfully wry and a bit sarcastic.

In this one particular episode they discuss being single by first saying that it really is no big deal, except for holidays. Holidays and weekends. Holidays and weekends and almost every day of the week. They end their conversation by agreeing that being single on Tuesdays is acceptable. Yes, on Tuesdays, it was perfectly fine to be single.

The exchange between these two characters made me laugh; it also was spot on.

One of the cruelest adjustments I faced when becoming suddenly single was what to do with my weekends. It was hard enough to figure out how to spend my hours during the week, but the cruelty came when there was no reward at the end of the week.

Instead of a reward, there is an unfathomable emptiness that accentuates just how alone you are. Being thankful for Friday turns into dreading Friday.

I wonder if people pick another partner quickly after a divorce or death because they simply cannot stand to be alone, especially on the weekends. I fought that temptation, but I do admit to an ache on Saturday night that has me longing for someone who has made a special plan for the evening.

When I began to emerge from the deep fog of sadness after my husband died, I learned to control my calendar. I make sure that there is something pleasant scheduled on the weekend so I don't wake up Saturday with the "I'm all alone blues." That something special could be just making sure that I've ordered a favorite movie to watch, planned a good dinner, or treated myself to a nice bottle of wine. The point is that I try to make sure I have something special to look forward to at the end of the week.

The surprising and pleasant side effect of confronting the cruelty of being alone on weekends resulted in making my weekends count for something, something almost always memorable. I've renewed friendships, I've kept in touch with family, I've taken advantage of cultural opportunities, and I've learned perhaps the most important lesson: learning to be still. I've tamped down my need to make "Thank God, It's Friday" holy.

Do I miss candlelight dinners with my husband and the buzz that comes from getting dressed for a special evening? Yes. I'm 65, but I feel like I still have the heart of an 18-year-old. I have to admit that this 65-year-old heart has been tested twice with tragedy, and while I am not a pessimist, I do not believe that the third time is a charm.

I still dislike the Saturday night syndrome. It took a long time and a lot of creative energy to make myself the social chair of my weekends. It is a job. It requires focus and hard work. I really don't like the job and I've been tempted many times to quit. Weekends reveal for the single person — at least for me — just how desirable it is to want to be taken care of or complimented. I miss the affirmation that comes with the phrase "you look nice tonight."

The longing gets less, and maybe someday it will finally disappear. But I doubt it. I've learned to accept that weekend management is simply a part of the becoming single evolution and when the longing appears, I force myself to focus on the advantages of the company I wish to keep, realizing I rarely have to do anything out of obligation.

Controlling your calendar is more empowering than controlling the television remote; it's just not as easy. It takes hard work, discipline and acceptance.

The Money

"...for richer, for poorer, in sickness
and in health, until death do us part."

This phrase, which comprises the heart of the marriage vows, is often spoken by couples who are participating in the most fairytale moment of their lives.

I've said these vows twice. I lived them to the best of my ability.

The vow "in sickness and in health" was tested to the limit with Larry. In both marriages, I didn't have to test the extreme aspects of "richer or poorer," nor did I fully understand the pivotal role money played in each marriage.

When my children were five and two-and-a-half years old, I started a career. I was 27, the year was 1973, and I was impressed with the feminist voices encouraging women's independence. I wanted my own paycheck.

By the time I was divorced eight years later, I was managing the equivalent of a small advertising agency. As a part of accepting my new single status, I did several things.

The first was to reclaim my maiden name. It was not a rebellious gesture; it was prompted by the fact that I felt my married name no longer applied.

I held fast to the feminist credo, trying hard to echo Helen Reddy, "I am woman hear me roar." My roar turned into a growl when my application for a credit card was denied by three different banks. They were denied because all of my assets had been jointly held with my husband. My income apparently didn't matter. What mattered was that I had no individual credit record.

I eventually solved the problem by pursuing and getting approved for an American Express card. It established me as a bona fide credit-worthy person. I have been an American Express card holder since 1981. Through my financial tumult over the past 31 years, I have assiduously guarded that relationship.

It isn't easy for me to summarize my relationship with money. All I know is that it plays a critical role in my life. I know I have been influenced by my parents and that our life as a family was governed by the ups and downs of our financial fortunes. I felt the fear of what we could not afford.

I developed an uneasy relationship with money. I was at once feisty and fearful. I was feisty when I demanded to be paid professionally for what I was worth in every job I was offered. I was fearful when I realized that keeping financially fit is no sure thing. Here today, gone tomorrow.

A review of my financial history reveals the following: At times, I borrowed more than I could afford. At times, I was flush with surplus income. At times, I wondered how I would pay the mortgage, medical bills, and the end-of-the-month expenses. In short, my relationship with money is checkered.

My mother used to quote Benjamin Franklin by saying, "Experience is a dear teacher, but fools learn by no other." At times, I was a fool, but my experiences made me wiser.

This I know:

Debt overwhelms serenity.

No matter how busy or how plagued by problems you are, know your financial situation.

Live by the rule: Better in my bank account than in someone else's.

Spend money on things that yield long-term pleasure — financial nutrition — multigrain versus white bread.

Figure out a budget. This can be really awful, but there isn't any other way to achieve a healthy relationship with money.

Learn the language of money. Learn the basics and hire someone you trust to handle the complicated issues.

Money can buy happiness as long as it is not tinged with greed.

My husband died in 2002 at the bottom of the dot com market crash. Our savings and investment accounts had been ravaged.

I shepherded the proceeds from his life insurance policy carefully. I became a student learning the language of money and investments. The economy was beginning to recover and I made some good investments. I call the years between 2003 and 2007 the "wahoo years."

In late 2007, I was blindsided by the perfect financial storm. The Great Recession gutted my investment accounts and I watched helplessly as my largest asset, my condo, dramatically declined in value. My financial outlook was bleak.

I had to look the tiger in the eye.

I constructed a stringent budget with the help of my financial advisor, Robin Bullard Carter, whose guidance I sought weeks after Larry died. If there were a stronger word than stringent, I would use it. The budget was predicated on saving my condo. It had become my safe haven.

I stuck religiously to the budget until the day I bought a case of wine, a modestly priced wine. But the purchase was not in my budget; I had buyer's remorse.

That case of wine made me realize I had to sell my condo to regain my sense of financial serenity.

Shortly after I put the condo on the market, I made another decision. Part of my learning to speak the language of money involved reading blogs and commentaries by financial experts. I gained valuable knowledge as a result and during the "wahoo years" I managed to make some good investments, but in 2009, I lost all of my confidence to trust my ability to navigate the maelstrom. I never gamble, but I realized that under the circumstances, if I continued to believe that I could pick a winning stock or bond, that's exactly what I would have been doing: gambling.

Panic seized me. My father had been burned badly by entrusting his money to experts, and he got swindled. I didn't know to whom I could turn, but I knew I had to do something because my bank accounts were hemorrhaging money.

I needed an expert. Robin Bullard Carter did not sell anything; she provided financial education and counseling. I did have an old family friend and a dear friend who are financial wizards; they both would have been happy to help me. But I could not pin my financial health on my friends. I needed someone whose opinions I trusted, but whose advice was on a strictly business level. I needed someone who had a handle on the big financial picture, someone who had the wisdom to see the whole reel as the recession was unfolding. Of all the experts who had unknowingly tutored me for six years, I admired David Kotok, head of Cumberland Advisors.

I lived by the credo that no one was going to wake up every morning worrying about Connie Wilder's money more than Connie Wilder. I had to face the fact that I had to turn that worry over to someone who knew how to worry productively. I took a giant leap of faith. With a good deal of chutzpah, I wrote to David Kotok.

Never in a million years did I imagine that David Kotok would answer the email that I wrote to him on a Sunday afternoon, summarizing my plight. But he did, five hours after I wrote it. He accepted me as a client. My nest egg is not large, but it is in the best incubator that I can imagine, and I'm grateful.

The platitudes of not living beyond your means and

"waste not, want not" are worth adopting. Living them is damn hard. But not sleeping at night is harder.

I've figured out that diets and budgets are pretty much the same. I weigh myself every day and check my account balances frequently. If either gets out of whack, I put on the breaks. This habit also allows me to occasionally have a big piece of lemon meringue pie and to buy a case of good wine without feeling guilty.

The Aging

I came back. I came back to Wellfleet to see what I had left behind. I came back in January, ten years later, to see the deserted beaches and the shuttered shops. I came back to look at the house, the house that sold within a half hour of being listed on the Internet. There was no time to even put a sign on the lawn.

I came back to the house I fled from less than six months after my husband died.

I came back to see the red door, now streaked from the wind. I peered over the small hedge, carefully avoiding stepping onto private property to see the herb garden, now overgrown. The lamp post still stood sturdy, but the window shades were drawn so it didn't look like there was anyone inside to turn on the lights. The wrought iron flower hook on which I always hung the first flowers of spring was still to the right of the door.

I stood for a while, staring at what was to have been our retirement home. This is where we were going to live our "out years" as my husband called them.

I left the house, because I could not live there without him. I could not carry out our dream that was damaged by his death.

Ten years later, I thought about, for the first time, whether we, together, could have lived our dream comfortably as we aged. Summers would have bustled with family and friends. But the roads are barely passable in summer, bearing the load of vacationers and the swell of seasonal help. Navigating them would have required a sharp mind and rapid reflex. Would we have had those in our "out years?"

In winter, the roads would not be congested, but there was no happy medium. Clear roads and the absence of clamoring tourists revealed an emptiness and a mordant scene.

I left the house at 55; I was standing in front of it now, ten years later, at 65.

We bought the house when I was 43 and my husband was 48. What were we thinking? We were smitten with the idea of spending our retirement years in an historic seaside town in a charming, antique, quintessential Cape Cod home, which we lovingly modernized.

Our hearts were young, our hopes were fresh and we were guided by romantic dreams of a future growing older together. What mattered to us in our 40s bore little resemblance to what we would need to survive comfortably in our 60s and beyond. We counted on our companionship to keep us happy. We counted on good health, sound bodies, and alert minds. We looked forward to sharing our 60s, 70s, 80s, and beyond together.

When Larry hatched the plan of buying the Cape house, he asked me a series of questions:

Did I want to retire to Florida? No, that was too retirement-like.

Did I want to retire to Maine? No, that was too desolate in winter.

What about Wellfleet? He didn't wait for me to answer; he framed the advantages for me. Wellfleet was near Boston; it was part of the beautiful, protected National Seashore; it had a vibrant arts community and historic significance; and it was full of charm.

Shortly after that conversation, which took place in summer, we bought our retirement home, believing we had asked ourselves and answered all the right questions about where to spend our "out years."

But what I knew to consider in my forties bore little similarity to what to consider in my 60s. Beaches and historic charm only matter as a place to live a senior life if it is also near a good hospital, near family, and architecturally accessible.

Standing at age 65, looking at our retirement home, and thinking about our decision made a little more than twenty years earlier, I finally realized that this was never the right home for us. Why? Because I have gone to school in the intervening years, studying what sliding into proper aging is all about.

In a nutshell, what matters is preserving independence. What matters are details clearly overlooked when romancing the aging process, when choosing where to live to support the senior years. Details like ease of rubbish and snow removal; landscape maintenance; having an attached garage; security systems, including medical and burglar alerts; as well as fire sprinkler systems, zoned heating, and air conditioning systems; convenient health care resources; and a sense of community.

In the Wellfleet house alone, I discovered how cruel winter months could be for a recently widowed woman in her mid-fifties. It turns out that facing that stark reality forced me to flee a situation that would have become more miserable. The surprise discovered by coming back ten years later was that, quite possibly, Larry's and my dream of a charmed retirement would have been sabotaged even if we had lived the dream together.

Standing and facing the house, relief overcame regret.

Larry died believing in the dream. He was spared the reality of understanding that aging requires acceptance of letting go of previously-imagined dreams and accepting new ones that may be far less romantic but which are based on nurturing true happiness.

I want to age. I want to figure out how to accept letting go of a certain vanity and replacing it with a new set of skills. I desperately want to age, and I want to be really good at it.

Looking at our house, I concluded that it would have hindered our aging rather than supported it. I thought how much maintenance it would have required to preserve the dignity of this antique house. How long would we have been able to back out of the driveway onto Wellfleet's Main

Street and not been broadsided by an oncoming car coming up the hill? Who would have been our neighborhood friends, when we were surrounded by beautiful churches and summer shops and galleries? How much of our monthly budget would have been absorbed by supporting the house, instead of supporting living things, like us?

How many times would we have been able to see our children and grandchildren? We would have missed so many little, but important, events like school plays, weekly dinners, and visits within reach. Larry died believing in our originally conceived dream; I am living the substitute dream that could not be fulfilled in our house.

I bolted from the house based on my instincts, knowing I was doing the right thing, but sadly knowing that I was abandoning a dream. Ten years later, the dream unraveled before my eyes.

The Decade

Ten years later, I am still standing, living a very different life from the one I pictured as a young girl. I thought that I would grow old with a loving husband, that we would enjoy the fruits of our life together and help each other face the inevitable changes as we aged.

It didn't turn out that way. Ironically, I think I am stronger than that young girl would have imagined. Because of my experiences and decisions made as the result of them, I believe I am in a better position to make my aging years more comfortable and productive.

I'm Medicare age now. The years between 55 and 65 have been good to me. Not easy, but good. I took a crash course in life management. I learned to speak the language of money; I focused on my health; I discovered how I liked to spend my time and how I didn't; I invented a new way to judge my accomplishments; I concentrated on nurturing cherished relationships; I created a living environment that suited my advancing years; and I tried, each day, to see the world around me as beautiful.

The dream I swapped from growing old with my husband was the new dream of becoming a whole and independent person.

Over the last ten years, I tested my ability to travel alone and to appreciate places that I thought I could only share with my husband. Museums, playhouses, movie theaters, restaurants, country roads, and busy cities were just some of the places I learned to share with myself. My world expanded when I did those things.

Now, I've shrunk my world; I've pared down my living environment. When I sold the house in Wellfleet, I moved to a large condo with a huge basement. It was perfect at the time. When the movers came to take my things to this new condo, one of the men, upon entering the house, said, "Ah, the woman with many boxes." He was right. I packed up all of my memories, knowing they would have a home until I could decide what to physically do with them.

Seven years later, I unpacked the boxes and went through the gut-wrenching process of what to save, what to give away and what to throw out. It was hard work. I sifted through years of photographs, documents, and letters. The sight of my husband's very distinctive handwriting was very hard to bear. My 97-year-old mother had recently died, and her records were also a part of this emotional exercise. As difficult as this process was, I kept telling myself that it was better that I was doing this now, rather than leaving the task to my children later.

My days are different too. I calculated recently that I spend about 80% of my time alone. That's a rather staggering percentage, but because of the expanded communication resources available to me, I have company most of the day.

Ten years ago, I wondered how I would ever learn to be alone, day in and day out. By the time my husband died, I was semi-retired, so I no longer went to the office during the day; my hours were my own to organize. I just had no idea what I was going to do with them. So many perplexing and even frightening questions filled my head.

Would I be bored?

Would I develop bad habits, like not eating enough or eating too much?

Would I drink too much?

Would I ever be able to sleep through the night again?

Would I have a sense of purpose?

Would I be able to keep my mind alert, when most of my conversations during the day would be in my head?

Would my health now suffer, because I had taken care of someone else for so long? Would I know how to take care of myself?

Would I be able to make major decisions alone, such as managing money and negotiating business matters, such as mortgages and insurance?

It turns out that confronting all of those fears over the last ten years has strengthened my resolve to appreciate my life. I take nothing for granted. I didn't know when I was figuring out the answers to those troubling questions that I was learning how to age gracefully: independently and with hope.

In moving "Beyond Wellfleet," I have embraced the new dream, the one I adopted when my husband died. I wanted to continue to see the world around me as beautiful and to become a whole person.

At my husband's funeral, which was attended by over 600 people (he was a public person, in addition to being incredibly loved and respected), I had to give his eulogy. Because he was loved by so many friends, if one person had been chosen, many others would have been hurt. If all had been encouraged to praise him at his funeral, we would have been in the church for hours. Only the children, the priest, and I spoke during the service.

I drew my remarks from the introduction of Homer's *Odyssey* which came from my father's text book when he was a student at Andover Academy. My husband and I used to send out "Odyssey Updates" to our friends and family during the four years of his cancer experience. For the last days of his life, he was so weak he could barely walk. He worked so hard to stay alert, but conversation was tiring for him. I needed to find a way for us to be together, but not to ask too much of his limited energy. I decided to read to him. I asked him if he would like me to read *The Odyssey* to him. We had to admit to each other that while we knew the story, neither of us had read the book. The memory of sitting at the end of our bed, reading to him, is both sweet and stinging.

The book proved to be more than just a way for us to be quietly together during his last days; it also inspired my eulogy. In the book's introduction, I found just the right words to describe my husband. They were words used to summarize Odysseus's character, and they were a perfect description of my husband:

*"When Man and Gods were arrayed against him, he faced them
with cool intelligence, patient courage, and a tenacious heart."*

That is the man I have learned to live without. I still miss him. I feel his presence when a strong breeze brushes my cheek or when I hear Ella Fitzgerald sing, or when I see a wave crash on his favorite beach in Wellfleet. He still resides in a corner of my heart. He left a vibrant echo.

But in the last ten years, I have learned to develop my own voice. It started as a whisper, but it grows stronger every day.

Acknowledgments

How do I adequately thank friends, family and strangers who have kindly loved, inspired, and held me close to their hearts? Impossible! The love has always been greater than my words of gratitude could convey. Each name on this list is etched on my heart and to those whose names I never knew, thank you.

Traci Harmon-Hay, whose painting changed my life

Porter Shreve, who wrote a comment, that I read every day, on my workshop essay at the Key West Literary Seminar

David R. Kotok, for his kindness and financial genius

Carol Courneen, who read every chapter I wrote and gave me the courage to keep going

Dottie Serdenis, my "agent," who commanded that I write a book

Pattie McCarthy, who read the stories when I was at my most vulnerable

Joni Annas Vetne, the editor (now friend) who polished my words

Kristine Steinberg, who expertly guided me onward

Gretchen Shields McClure, who took a gorgeous painting and created a dazzling cover

The therapists who saved my sanity

The Key West Literary Seminar, where I was introduced to a world of wonderful writers

The Novelistas who make my every day: Carol Courneen, Sherrie Loveman, Sam Rounds

The Siblings who love their sister—John and Claire Turner; Deane and Gudrun Turner; Priscilla and William Ambrose; Tommy Wilder; and close-to-brother, Sam Cady

The Ants, who carried us on their backs: Patty and Jerry Adduci, Posy Cameron and Bob Brothers, Jan and Tom Fink, Pattie McCarthy, Joann Milam, Betsy and Howard Relin, Dottie Serdenis, Janet and Ethan Welch, Bobbie Wilson

The Cheering Squad, who encouraged me to keep writing: Patty Adduci, Lynn and Bill Case, Claudia Harris, Gloria Healy, Marilynn Dowd, Gretchen Maguire, Annie Potter, Jill Ryan

My Other Family: Janet and Ethan Welch

The Complementary family: Bob James, Rev. Janet James, Amanda James

My favorite writing places: Café San-Malo, Emerson Inn By the Sea, Hotel Dominion 1912, Mount Washington Inn, Pier 77, Scargo Café, Seaglass, Stellas, Wentworth By the Sea, Wicked Oyster, Windsor Arms, The Bedford Inn, The Mayflower Inn, The Red Lion Inn, The Studio at Old Comfortable

To all those who greeted my black book and me warmly, especially Kayla at Wellfleet's Wicked Oyster; she understood the story of where it all began — at a corner table at the Outer Cup

And the Last shall not be Least: Katie, Rob, David, Staci, Sebastien, Ethan and Bobby

www.ingramcontent.com/pod-product-compliance
Lightning Source LLC
Chambersburg PA
CBHW030028290326
41934CB00005B/541